Reflections

Thru My

Windshield

(Part One)

by Dave Madill

Reflections Thru My Windshield

First Edition October, 2005

For more information contact:
Write Up The Road Publishing
P.O. Box 69
Kenton, TN 38233
(800) 292-8072
www.writeuptheroad.com

Madill, David R.
Reflections Thru My Windshield (Part One)

ISBN: 0976687216
Library of Congress Control Number: 2005931805

A Write Up The Road Book
Printed in the United States of America

Dedication

Dedicated to every trucker who ever turned a wheel
and to their families and loved ones
that support them.

A special dedication to Betty, (My Wife),
and my children who have supported me while
I traveled across the two greatest nations
on the face of the earth.

Dave

Best wishes

Barry.

Dave Madill

08/25/07

Table of Contents:

My Bear

I wander slowly through my mind
    to a time without care
When I was but a little child, my best friend was a bear.

A bear so soft and fluffy; buttons were his eyes
Together we would wander where dragons ruled the skies.

Many were our adventures as we wandered there.
I began to wonder what happened to that bear,

The innocence of a child lost in the sands of time
Yet somehow I still visit there, memories in my mind

Is there a place for innocence in the hustle of our life
Is there a place for childhood dreams,
    in the midst of all this strife;

That little corner of my life, my mind still
    wanders there
One thing that still bothers me; where did I leave that bear.

Fallen Angel

A lady with big blue eyes and a body made for love
Tonight soon we will fly to the moon and stars above
I'll gently take her in my arms and kiss her pretty lips
My hands begin to wander from her shoulders to her hips.

Slowly I'll undress her and lead her to my bed;
Cover her with kisses from her toes up to her head
Our questing hands are busy; they slowly light the fire
Hungrily our bodies join, our passion spirals higher.

But I know I'll never hold her, except here in my dream.
Tonight again I'll make love to her,
        asleep here in my dream.
In my dreams she joins me, we touch the stars above:
This little angel and me share a night of love.

When that little angel joined me in my bed:
Even as our bodies joined, she crept into my head
Her body young and tender, her kisses sweet like wine -
Long hair upon my pillow, pictures in my mind.

This lady sweet and gentle, with a heart so full of love
So much like an angel, came down from up above
This angel fell from heaven and joined me in my bed
Now my fallen angel is in my heart as well as my head.

Whispering Wind

The wind whispers in the pines,
 small branches gently sway.
The wind seems to call to me,
"Come with me and play -

Dance with me among the trees,
skip across the mountain high
Gently swirl across the lake
and chase clouds across the sky."

The wind whispers to my mind,
"Come with me and play."
Yet I am but an earth bound man:
grounded I must stay.

Yet still my mind may wander,
and dance among the trees
Soaring with the whispering wind,
my soul and mind are free.

Just a Kiss

I stumble slowly from the truck each joint and muscle sore
Then I see her standing there, waiting there at the door.

I smell of dirt and diesel; somehow, she does not care
I feel her press her lips to mine, feel her fingers
       through my hair.

Then seated at the table, she brings me up to date
Everything that has happened while I have been away.

As I sit and listen, I watch her gentle smile
How do I deserve this woman who waits mile after mile.

I listen as she tells me how the children, they have grown
And the many things that happened since
       the last time I was home.

She is the reason that I keep working
       and why I live like this
How can I tell her of my love; I stop her with a kiss.

Holding You

Three thousand miles away from home,
      but tonight I'll hold you tight.
You are with me in my dreams each and every night.

I feel your body next to mine; your scent is in the air
Tenderly I hold you tight, run my fingers through your hair.

Somehow my spirit joins with yours
      throughout the long, dark night
Then flies back to its lonely bed in the early morning light.

Even when I am far from home, my darling, do not weep
Remember that I am holding you, as we lie fast asleep.

Woman

Why is that a woman's touch, can stop a child's cry

Why is it that a woman's smile, seems to clear the sky

Why is that a woman's tears, can melt the coldest heart

Why is it that a woman's kiss, can tear your world apart

Why is it that a woman's laugh, seems to calm a stormy sea

Why is it that a woman's love, can bring a strong man
    to his knees

What is this power a woman holds, that shines so like a sun

I probably will never know, but I love them every one.

Homecoming

Twelve thousand miles in four weeks' time;
        now I'm close to home
The one I love is waiting there; we just got off the phone

Tonight I'll take her in my arms and hold her
        'til dawn's light
We will be together; there will be no tears tonight.

My big old diesel rumbles, the miles are flying by
Now I can see the lights of home reflected in the sky.

Now I pull into the yard and shut that old diesel down,
Draw a line in the logbook and take one last look around.

As I walk into the house, I am greeted at the door
Two kids, two dogs, a cat and the one I'm looking for,

Greeted by my family with a great big "Daddy's home!"
Do the children realize how we want to be alone

But that must wait 'til later, our time alone can wait
Right now it is the children's turn to bring me up to date.

I hear about their friends at school, the teachers
        that they like,
How Mummy took them swimming, how Junior
        broke his bike,

                                    ...

...

Several hours later the children are in bed.
She shyly slips her hand in mine; she leads me to our bed.

Our bodies press together, our clothes lay scattered
        on the floor
She whispers how much she missed me; a child knocks on
        our bedroom door:

Two children come into the room, two little sleepy heads,
Crying how much they missed their daddy
        as they climb into our bed.

My family all around me; our time alone must wait
Oh, god, here come the dogs - isn't family life great.

Predator

Am I prey or hunter here in this jungle scene,
Even nature is my enemy on this field of dappled green;
Even shadows seem to move and my clothes are
      soaked in sweat,
Damn this god-forsaken hell; why must it be so wet,
Motionless I crouch here; I hardly seem to breathe
My senses all on high alert, I scan among the leaves.

Slowly I move forward; here I must take my time,
Both hunter and hunted; my life is on the line.
When I return to the world and to my folks at home
Will they be proud of me, of how my mind has grown,
Will they notice how I've changed from
      what I was back then:
I am only what they made me: a predator of men.

Mistake

She pulled into the truck stop in a big shiny cab-over Pete,
Her long legs were a sight to see as she climbed down
     from the seat.
She looked just like a model, her dress, her form, her face -
Not the usual type of woman that you see around this place.

She walked across the pavement in that dress
     so short and red,
Every single man among us had visions of a bed.
You could have heard a pin drop when she walked
     through that door,
Every eye was on her as she wiggled across the floor.

Straight up to the counter and in a voice both deep and low,
Said: "Where the hell's the men's room –
     this cat has to go!"
The diner was pure bedlam as we departed from the scene:
     our vision in a red dress
     was a darn ol' pavement queen!

Who Choose

I have stood among the crosses of those who went before,
I have stood amid the carnage and heard the cannons roar.

The crying of the wounded, the silence of the dead
It made me stop and wonder: it could be me instead.

Who is it that does the choosing; one to live and one to die.
I know among the fallen are much better men than I.

So I salute the heroes who have paid the final price,
Some day I hope to join them
        around the throne of Jesus Christ.

The Rookie

We heard him top that mountain pass;
the brakes began to squeal

He headed down that six percent,
hands clenched upon the wheel

Smoke was coming from the back
by the time he hit the level,

The color of his brake drums
would have even pleased the devil.

Sweat was pouring from his brow
when he pulled off to the side,

He shook his head in wonder
and said "Man, what a ride!"

His trainer said, "You did OK;
you kept it on the road,

But the next time we come over here,
we have to pull a load."

Our Night

I reach out and take her hand,
strange thoughts run thru my head
Clothes lie scattered on the floor,
she leads me to her bed.

Her hair spreads across the pillow;
our lips and tongues entwine
Her body sets me afire,
her kisses taste like wine.

My hands caress her body;
gently I part her thighs
My mouth wanders over her body;
I hear her gentle cries.

My lips now find her center;
my tongue finds a new home
She slowly writhes in ecstasy;
I hear her begin to moan.

Now I move, she straddles me,
her knees beside my waist
Gently now our bodies join,
there is no time to waste.

Our bodies move in unison,
even faster is our speed
I reach up and caress her breasts,
I feel her every need.

...

...

I feel her body tremble;
I join her with my release
She lies back down beside me,
our bodies now at peace.

Gently now I hold her,
my lust so much like a flame:
Quiet for the moment,
but it will flare up again.

All through the darkness of the night
our bodies join in love
No one sees our pleasure
but a big old moon above.

The Journey

The road lies there ahead of you and it's uphill all the way
There are friends and others who will help you on the way

Slowly turn and look behind, across the sands of time
Those footprints on the road you walked,
       some of them were mine.

Many times my trail has wandered and I have gone astray
I've wandered in the darkness for many lonely days.

I have wandered down the alleys, I've stumbled and I fell
I have seen the worst of life, touched the very gates of hell.

Yet even in my darkest hour, in the long and lonely night,
Someone came and rescued me and led me
       towards the light.

So if you ever stumble, just reach out and take my hand
You see, we are all connected in the brotherhood of man.

It's a long old road ahead of you, and yes,
       it's uphill all the way
Together we can make it, if we take life day by day.

My Stand

I hear the sound of distant drums and I can hear
      the bugle cry
The time has come for me to go, and fight; perhaps to die,

I will not fight for money, for glory or for fame
I will not fight another because our gods aren't the same.

I will fight for freedom, for that I will take up a gun
I will not lay it down again until the battle has been won.

For justice and for liberty, for that I'll take a stand
The right to live the way I choose in this or any land.

If people wish to learn and grow, then freedom is a need
In the tree of knowledge, freedom is a seed.

For freedom we must stand on guard,
      answer the bugle's call
The time has come for us to fight and some of us will fall.

If I should not return to you, tell the children that I tried
Tell them I held freedom's torch even as I died.

Those who have died for freedom let us not forget
For when we march to battle, they will be with us yet.

The legacy they leave us when the battle has been won,
Will carry on forever: freedom for everyone.

Medicine Woman

She has crossed the snowcapped Rockies,
trod upon the grassy plains
Walked lush and peaceful valleys
and seen the desert bloom with rain.

Her spirit, like an eagle,
has reached out to touch a cloud
Swum waters with the salmon
beneath a waterfall so loud.

She saw the eagle in his mating flight,
heard the elk, his bugle call
Seen flowers in the springtime,
picked dry weeds in fall.

She knows of herbs and grasses
and other healing things
Learned about the wilderness
and the healing nature brings.

She's a modern medicine woman
who can help you with your pain
Then she goes back to her mountain,
which makes her whole again.

The Eagle

I've studied the sands of time;
seen history unfold
The rise and fall of nations,
their people proud and bold.

Rivers have run red with blood as nations came to life
Brother fought with brother in man's eternal strife.

Now I hear the eagle scream; awake my sons, arise
Our nation is in turmoil; trouble fills the skies.

The tree in which I built my nest,
the branch on which I stand
Is being torn asunder
by politicians' hands.

Our freedom is in jeopardy as they try to still my voice
They put a cage around me and my right to make a choice.

This tree planted by Madison and others of his band
Grown straight by the grace of God; for liberty it stands.

Arise, my sons and daughters.
You must defend this tree!
Washington and all his friends knew
Eagles must be free.

Jesus Wept

It was a cold and lonely highway
about a thousand miles from home
The night was dark and stormy;
I was out there all alone.

The thunder rolled like cannon fire,
the lightning danced like flame
I thought someone was calling
and I swore I heard my name.

Just then the lightning struck
a tall and stately tree
And left there was a giant cross
for all the world to see.

Frightened, I pulled over
and got down on my knees to pray
I knew my life was over;
I had reached my Judgment Day.

Then once more the lightning flashed
a clear and perfect light,
And suddenly before me
stood our Saviour Jesus Christ

And now I knew I heard a voice,
a voice so sweet and clear
Then as I looked up towards him
I saw him shed a tear.

...

...

He said "Your life, it is not over;
your soul, it is not lost.
For I forgave the sins of man
when I died upon the cross."

Then suddenly around me
I felt his boundless love,
Gathered close around me
as his tears fell from above.

He said "Arise, O sinner man,
and live your life for me."
Then another bolt of lightning
turned the cross back to a tree.

Now I'm out here on the highway,
my sinful soul set free
My life I gave to Jesus
the night the Saviour wept for me.

At Peace

I wander among the mountains,
land of Eagle, Deer and Bear
A harsh and unforgiving land,
man is a stranger there.

Many men have lost their lives
trying to tame this land
Their bones lie on the forest floor
scattered by nature's hand.

Somehow I am welcome here,
I feel no trace of fear
I stand among the pines;
I stop and watch the Deer.

An Eagle soars above me
on currents in the sky
A Cougar crouches in the rocks
as I go passing by.

A Grizzly stops his fishing:
he never makes a sound
A mighty Wolf stands watchfully;
can I be on hallowed ground?

At peace I stand among the crags
and I feel the cool wind blow
I look down on the works of man
in the valley far below.

The Big Rig

There's a tale out on the highway, a legend I've been told
About a rig that's made of silver, with wheels of solid gold
There's crosses on the mud flaps, and if you look inside
Jesus does the driving with St. Peter by his side.
I seen them once in Texas, and another time in Maine
Once on roads of ice and snow, and another time in rain
I know they took a side trip, just to help me find my road
And proudly I'll go with them
      when I've pulled my final load.

As I travel down life's highway, I'll do the best I can
I know that I'm not perfect; after all I'm just a man
I know that I'm not perfect: I've cheated and I've lied
But God, he is forgiving, and he knows that I've tried.
I've cheated on my logbooks but God knows that's no sin,
With Jesus as my Saviour, I know they'll let me in
So I'll travel down life's highway and
      when I pull that final mile
When Jesus stops to pick me up, I'll greet him with a smile.

I'll ask if I can drive that rig, with the wheels of solid gold
He'll toss me the keys and say,
      "My friend, you've earned this load."
Then heaven's gates will open wide,
      when they hear that air horn blast
And the final logbook entry reads,
      "The trucker's home at last."

Reach Out

Just reach out and take my hand, everything will be all right
Let me hold you close to me
        throughout the long dark nights.

Place your head upon my pillow;
        I will make your spirit sing
Let me show you the pleasure the act of love can bring.

As our bodies move together,
        your passion is my guiding light
To satisfy your every dream is my only wish tonight.

But I will not try to hold you when it's time for you to go
Kiss me as you are leaving; say my name as you turn to go.

There is no need to say a word, everything will be all right
Just reach out and take my hand and let me love you
        through the night.

Lovers

Her hair upon the pillow shines in the pale moonlight
Her body in the twilight glows with an inner light
Tenderly she reaches out and greets me with a kiss
My trembling fingers touch her skin and
           there is no more perfect bliss.

The moon slips behind a cloud, he shyly dims his glow
Lovers need their privacy; he will not watch this show
Gently we merge together, two hearts merge as one
Our bodies move together until the passion's done.

The moon slips out to take a peek and sees a lovely sight
Her head upon my shoulder, together in the night,
The moon in his entire splendor bathes us in his beams,
Two lovers in the darkness; together, with our dreams.

Shared Dream

You slipped into my dream last night
like smoke from a candle flame
You smiled and kissed me gently
and quietly called my name
Lost in the moment, I held you in my arms
I surrendered to the passion; a prisoner of your charms.

Then in a moment you were gone, like a thief into the night
You were gone when I awoke to see dawn's lonely light.
Your scent upon my pillow; a hint of perfume in the air
Was I only dreaming , or were you really there?

Join me in my dream tonight, beneath the pale moonlight,
Together in a dream we share, we will love away the night.

The Last Real Cowboy

A quiet little barroom in a little nameless town
Nowhere to go and time to kill, I suck a cold beer down
An old cowpoke ambles in the door
      and slowly looks around,
There's just the bartender and me,
      so he says, "I'll buy a round."

He saunters slowly across the floor,
      both bowlegged and pigeon-toed,
His legs still hold the memory of every horse he rode.
I thank him kindly for the beer as he sits down at the bar
He asks about my rig outside, and have I come very far;
We sit and talk for hours and he tells me about the range
He tells me about the cowboy life
      and the many things that have changed.

He says there are no real cowboys now, riding for the brand
He talks about the life he had and makes it sound so grand.
He talks about the dusty trails
      and about some barroom fights
About rounding up the cattle and riding herd all night.

        ...

...

He tells me about the rustlers
      and his old Colt forty-four,
Now it hangs on a wall at home,
      he don't pack a gun no more.
I told him about the trucking life and the long, lonely roads
The many places I had been and the many heavy loads.
Finally he got up to leave, and I stood to have my say,
I said, "There is one real cowboy left,
      I just met him today."

He slowly turned and looked at me,
      grinned and shook my hand,
Said, "I'd be proud to have a man like you
      working for our brand."

Now I've been back there many times,
      across that old barroom floor,
I never met my friend again;
      he doesn't come there anymore.
You see, he's up there riding on the big range in the sky,
Now there are no real cowboys left,
      the last of them has died.

Blizzard

Winter on the prairies and the road is white with snow
The sky has turned to dark gray
    and the wind begins to blow,

Snow flies across the highway and drifts begin to grow
Telephone poles disappear, obscured by blowing snow.

My speed along the highway slows down to a crawl
My lights are almost useless, I can hardly see at all,

Suddenly in the darkness I see the exit sign
The truck stop is a mile ahead; my trip will work out fine.

I pull into the truck stop, back my truck into a row
Snow sweeps across my hood;
    listen to that cold wind blow,

Then I crawl into my bunk to rest my weary head
Lay there as the old truck rocks, as I lay warm in my bed.

Morning comes and I awake to see a different sight
Mother Nature changed the scene,
    in the middle of the night,

Where once there was a row of trucks
    is now drifted six feet high
Where once there was a roadway, no cars are going by.

...

...

I stumble to the café; I'll sit and wait this out
Wait for the plows and sanders to come and plow us out,

Then Old Man Winter takes a break
      and the sun begins to shine,
Winter's fury has moved on further down the line.

Faith

Another lonely truck stop, another lonely night
Just got off the telephone; my family is all right.
The waitress pours me coffee and I tell her a little joke
I sit there at the counter with a coffee and a smoke.

I hear the drivers talking about families and home
And the life that we are living on the highways all alone.
But something keeps me going and helps me pay the price:
My faith in God Almighty and our Saviour Jesus Christ.

I know they will protect me and help the ones I love,
Until the day they take me to that truck stop up above.

Promised Land

Up above the normal crowd in my steed of glass and steel,
The rhythm of my heart beats
     with the pounding of the wheels,
My diesel sings a happy note as the highway winds along,
It seems to say, "We're nearly home,"
     with the rumble of its song.

We pull into the driveway and our song begins to die,
I turn the key and shut it down,
     the engine seems to sigh
I step down slowly from the cab
     and she meets me at the door
As I put my arms around her,
     now I know what I'm working for:

She greets me with a tender kiss and takes me by the hand
I know my run is over; I have reached the Promised Land.

What Happened

The truckers on the highways,
    common folk like you and me,
They are what keeps the nation running
    and what helps keep it free,

You will never see a lawyer, out tying down a load,
Never see a politician four weeks on the road,
Why will they never listen to anything we say?
What happened to democracy; has it been thrown away?

Somehow there must be a way
    for us to have a voice,
The time has come, my many friends,
    for us to make the choice.

Partners

Two big rigs in the darkness
running hard through the night,

Headlights burning brightly
cut a tunnel through the night,

Two drivers, each in their cabs,
a father and a son,

Thunder down the highway
on another midnight run.

A father shares his wisdom:
thirty years out on the road,

Teach another generation
how to haul the heavy loads.

A different type of bonding
between this father and his son,

A partnership in diesel fumes
forged on a midnight run.

Superior Autumn

I drive along the highway along Lake Superior's shore,
The colors in the autumn, no man could ask for more
The beauty of the hardwoods touched
       by Mother Nature's hand,
Make me glad to be alive and to drive across this land.

I park – walk through the forest, to a beach by waters blue,
No painting can do justice to the beauty I walk through.
I stand in silent wonder and above I hear a cry
The lonely sound of wild geese
       winging south across the sky.

I know that if I die tonight and go on to Heaven's dream,
It will not match the majesty of Superior's autumn scene.

Little Ring

Sitting in a truck stop just the other night,
Tired, sad, and all alone; nothing was going right.
Talked to another driver, a pretty little thing,
It was plain that she was looking,
      wouldn't mind a little fling.

With all the drivers in there, she was interested in me
It gave my ego quite a boost; I'm rather plain, you see.
My mind told me to go ahead, and accept this little thing,
Then I picked up my coffee
      and on the counter saw a ring.

Just a simple ring of coffee made me think of you at home,
I left her at the counter and went to my truck alone.
You see that ring of coffee made me
      look down at my hand,
Even though I do not wear one, I saw a wedding band.

I remembered vows that I had made
      on the day that we were wed,
"Faithful to one another," were the very words we said.
Now, please don't worry about me
      when I'm on the road all alone,

Remember that I think of you, the one I left at home.

Truckers

What makes a man a trucker, why does he play this role?
Is the something deep inside him in his heart or in his soul?

The thunder of his diesel:
      does it fill an inner need,
What makes a man a trucker,
      are they a different breed -

Are a thousand lonely truck stops
      a substitute for home?
Does he think of wife and family while
      he's out there all alone.

The rhythm of the highway
      is a sad and lonely song,
And he dreams about his loved ones
      as the big rig moves along.

There is a touch of wanderlust that
      the highway helps to fill,
As he looks around the next bend,
      over another hill.

His family, they wait at home; he'll get back when he can,
That's what keeps him going, this special breed of man.

Freedom's Call

War clouds race across our land, a beast is on the prowl,

Death raises up his ugly head, we hear his mighty howl:

The nation's youngest and its best
        answer to the bugles' call,

To them will fall the fighting, and some of them will fall.

Parents of our nation; faster beat their hearts,

Sons and daughters march to war, families are torn apart.

As the battle rages, some of the best must fall

Families must pay the price to answer freedom's call.

Cry Freedom

Mother Freedom has been wounded, smoke rises
      around her like a cloud,

Bodies of her children lie covered by a shroud.

I hear the corpses calling, in their anger and their pain,

"We gave our lives for freedom - let us not die in vain."

Struck down by a coward's hand,
      in their innocence they died,

Freedom's torch they throw to you: hold this banner high.

We must always be vigilant; this is a price we must pay,

Or we will lose our freedom to a tyrant's will some day.

Stand on guard my brothers, stand tall and proud my sons,

Though we may pay an awful price, this battle will be won.

Rolling Thunder

From Halifax to old San Fran, from Tampa up to Nome,
There is a million miles of highway
    that the big rigs call their home.

If you stand beside that highway any time of night or day,
You can hear the rolling thunder
    as they pass along the way.

Cross mountains and cross desert with any type of load,
You know that they would roll through hell,
    if the devil built a road.

The thunder of the big rigs is the song of liberty,
And the drivers are the people that keep our nations free.

The freedom of our nations depends on hands of steel,
And one rests on the gearshift, and the other on the wheel.

The drivers of these big rigs are a special type of breed,
And the rhythm of the highway seems to fill an inner need.

The thunder of the diesel and the whining of the tires
Seems to set their blood to pumping,
    and set their souls on fire.

The cold and lonely blacktop just never seems to end,
And the rig that he is pushing
    becomes a driver's closest friend.

So come out to the highway and listen for the song,
The call of rolling thunder as the big rigs roll along.

Trucks of Steel

I learned to drive in harder times,
when trucks were made of steel,
Our seats were not cushions of air
and arms strong turned the wheel.

The Autocars and Brockways
have long since turned to rust,
The iron men that jammed the gears
are now no more than dust.

We changed our own tires then,
with pry bars and with sweat,
Our springs were blocks of rubber;
my back can feel it yet.

An open window kept you cool;
our pillow was a steering wheel,
Men were made of iron;
trucks were made of steel.

We were Knights in shining armor,
champions of the road,
Everyone respected us
as we pulled those heavy loads.

Then along came Hollywood
with films I will not name
Suddenly we were villains,
how much things have changed.

...

. . .

Trucks are made of plastic now,
we pull even bigger loads,
Drivers now get no respect
from others on the road.

I guess I am a dinosaur;
it's time for me to retire,
I'll dream about the trucks of steel
as I sit and watch the fire.

June

Three days out from Jersey on a west coast run
I went inside a country bar to have a little fun
Fiddles were a-playing, guitars were in tune
I spied a little lady and she said her name was June.

I asked that little lady to teach me how to dance
She slowly looked me up and down;
       said she'd take a chance.
She taught me how to two-step and how to Do-si-do
She taught me all the dances a country boy should know.

Then later on that evening, in her car down by the lake,
She taught me some other moves
       that country girl could make
That lady is now married and has a little son,
Tonight I'm coming home to her
       from another west coast run.

I love my little lady and I love our baby son,
Tonight me and that lady will have a little fun.
We'll go down to the honky-tonk, and I'll ask her to dance;
Later I will ask her to take another chance.

We'll hop in that old car again and drive down by the lake,
I'll see if she remembers the moves she used to make.
I love my little lady; yes I love my little June,
Tonight I'm going to take her on a second honeymoon.

Kiss This

DOT has shut me down, but I'm not even tired.
The company says to be on time or else you will be fired.

Shipper says to hurry up, but he took eight hours to load -
The company says I can make that up out there on the road.

They made me an appointment and tell me I can't be late;
I'm already four hours behind when I pull out of the gate.

Smokey says I drive too fast, and to back it off to fifty-five;
Dispatch says, You're running late;
       put your foot in it and drive.

I back my trailer to the dock, and I'm only two hours late,
Receiver says, "Don't sweat it, son, we don't need it
      'til next week."

The life of a long hauler sure is not filled with bliss.
I don't mind them screwing me;
      but I sure would like a kiss.

That Call

His coat came in the mail today; so she hung it in the hall,
One million miles safe driving and she's hoping
      he will call;

So many things to tell him about the dreams they share,
The baby tried to walk today; he wanted to be there.

The phone rings and she answers, but it isn't him that calls.
They said they were Highway Patrol from just below
      Great Falls.

A big rig there has overturned and the driver lost his life;
He swerved to miss a family car: two kids, husband
      and a wife.

From her trembling fingers the phone falls to the floor,
Her husband won't be coming home; she needs to hear
      no more.

She stumbles down the hallway and checks on
      three sleepy heads,
Walks into the bedroom and falls crying on the bed.

Crying, she hugs the pillow where he once laid his head,
Remembers all the hopes and dreams
      they hatched there in that bed.

Trucking is a hard life and many drivers live with pain,
But nothing like the pain she feels;
      her man won't be home again.

The Stranger

He walked into the diner, on his face a tired smile,
The lines etched on his face showed every weary mile.
He was slim and not too tall, and had started to turn gray
The hollows underneath his eyes showed the price
      that he had paid.

The waitress poured his coffee; she had seen
      his type before
She knew he was a driver before he hit the door.
He sat there sipping coffee and listened to us chin,
I knew that in a minute he would chip in.

The talk was all on trucking, the places that we had been,
The weird loads that we had hauled and
      people we had seen.
I saw the stranger give a start;
      Pete said he'd been everywhere;
Said he, "Hell's one place you haven't been;
      I know you ain't been there.

"Coming home one midnight, overweight and out of time,
I came around the corner, astride the yellow line:
I never even seen the car; it happened much too fast,
That ride took me down to hell: it was a fatal crash.

You see, what really happened on the midnight run,
I came around the corner and killed my wife and son."

You could have heard a pin drop as he walked out the door,
His footsteps echoed eerily as he walked across the floor.

                ...

...

We heard his diesel starting, but never saw him leave,
Just a shadow across the window and sulfur on the breeze.

Now, driver, you've done many things
        and you've been everywhere;
I'm hoping where that stranger went;
        you never will go there.

Northern Lights

Standing by the roadside I watch the Northern Lights,

Darkness folds around me, above me; a lovely sight

I watch in silent wonder a light show in the sky,

I do not even notice the time that passes by.

In silence still I stand there; I hear a different sound:

A hissing, crackling type of noise that
        comes from all around.

My mind is full of wonder, yet if I should die tonight,

I have seen the greatest show -
        I have heard the Northern Lights.

Endless Highway

Thirty years of driving on a highway without end
Another lonely truck stop is waiting around the bend
I'll joke and tease the waitress and talk to the other guys
We'll talk about conditions and tell a couple lies.

Then it's back to this old truck, the highway looms ahead
Sometime before tomorrow I'll spend some time in bed.

The highway never seems to stop,
            it goes on around the bend,
From east to west and north to south, it never seems to end.
Could there be a highway that leads to heaven's gates?
And maybe one that runs to hell,
            where the Devil sits and waits …

Let me take the right road, when it's time to make that ride,
 And have lots of room for parking,
            when I reach the other side.

Thirty years of driving on this highway with no end
Could there be a better truck stop
            somewhere around the bend?

A Trucker's Request

A woman walks beside me; we face life hand-in-hand

Without her I am nothing, with her I'm a man.

Together through our problems, we face life side by side

Until the day they take me upon my final ride.

I'll stand before the Final Judge, prepared to have my say,

I hope that he will understand what I ask for on that day.

My place here in the garden, I give it to my wife;

To make up for the many things she didn't have in life.

The many nights she sat alone and waited for my call,

The many things she did without, as I made another haul.

The many tears she cried while I was on the road,

The trials that she faced alone, while I pulled another load.

If I have earned some credit, in my time upon the earth

Please give it to the woman that gave my children birth.

A special type of woman who deserves a better life -

Oh, Lord, give her the best you have,
                    she is a trucker's wife.

One Year

A year for you has come and gone,
    look back on it with pride

All your toils and troubles,
    you took them in stride

Minutes felt like hours;
    a day felt like a year

A week was an eternity;
    yet you are standing here

The long road that awaits you,
    you do not face it alone

With God and friends beside you,
    I know you will make it home.

Gone Home

I left her at the graveside and walked
down to a little stream,
Sat beside a waterfall, its waters fresh and clean;

Over the rushing of the water,
a voice came from the air
In the gentle mist I saw her, the sunlight in her hair.

Her voice said, "Do not grieve, my son,
you are not left alone,
I've gone ahead to save your place;
our Father called me home."

The mist gathered around me and mixed
with the tears on my face
Her spirit all around
in the peace of this green place,

She said she would watch over me
from her place up above
Slowly I walked from that stream
filled with her perfect love.

I went back and joined my family,
my children and my wife,
My grieving time was over; we must get back to life.

Yet she is always with me,
I am not alone,
Someday I hope to join her when our Father calls me home.

Betty

Whenever I have stumbled, you were there to lend a hand
Whenever I have faltered, you helped me make a stand

When I needed something because the world
      had done me harm
I found both love and comfort, here within your arms.

I know you had your hopes and dreams,
but you put them aside
You took on another's problems,
when you became my bride.

Now we are growing older and our hair is turning gray
If you could do it all again, would you go another way?

Don't answer that last question, leave me my manly pride
It's enough that you are here tonight, sleeping by my side.

As I watch you sleeping, I wonder if you know
How very much my love has grown, from oh, so long ago.
I am like many other men, and I cannot speak of this
While you lie there sleeping. I will tell you with a kiss.

I do not want to wake you, for you might see my tears,
The tears I shed are happy ones,
      in thanks for all these years.

Highway Song

I drive along the highways, I listen to their song

A mix of very many styles, as the big rigs move along

A song about a cheating heart, blue eyes crying in the rain;

The diesel sings a sad note that adds to all the pain.

The rhythm of the drive wheels match the sobbing of a wife

Memories of a last kiss, when a driver lost his life.

The gear train adds a happy note at the ending of a run,

Another driver coming home to see his wife and son.

It would take Beethoven to tell about the strife;

Maybe add a little bit of Hank, to bring this song to life,

Mix in some of Eric's rock, and a sad and lonely horn;

Throw them all together and a highway sound is born.

Mere words cannot do justice: they can't describe the song

I hear out on the highway, as the big rigs roll along.

Phantom 1209

Midnight on the prairies: you can hear coyotes howl,

Somewhere on the interstate, a big rig's on the prowl,

The thunder of his engine sends a shiver through the night,
Darkness is ripped asunder by an eerie ghostly light.

I was out there on the highway, dog-tired and running late,

A load that had to be on time - sleep would have to wait.

From nowhere that rig passed me, and I blinked him
            back in line,
The name upon the back door was Phantom 1209.

I punched down on the throttle, to keep this rig in sight,

Someone that I could talk to, to help me through the night,

I heard over the radio, "I know you're short on time,
Hang on to my taillights; we will both get there on time."

All at once around me, I felt a kind of chill;

My rig was picking up some speed while going up a hill.

We talked to each other through the night
            on families and home,
And being on the highway, dog-tired and all alone,

...

...

And then I heard him tell me, "Your stop's a mile away."

And in the coming daylight, that rig faded away.

"If you're ever running late," I heard him give a call,
"Just ask for Phantom 1209; I'll help you make the haul."

Another lonely truck stop a few months down the line,

I told this tale about him; that Phantom 1209.

Some said I had been dreaming
as we drove those miles away,

But several older drivers nodded; and they smiled -

Then out there on the super slab,
        we heard the air horns blow,
And a big old diesel thundered by,
        with an eerie kind of glow...

I know that he is out there, helping drivers down the line,
He's out there on the Interstate, that Phantom 1209.

The Ballad of Texas Red

We were sitting at a truck stop a couple months ago;
A few of us old-timers: there was me, and Fred, and Joe,

And a guy that Joe was training;
they called him Texas Red,
He was an older trainee with lots of gray upon his head.

Now Red had spent about thirty years
stocking shelves in a grocery store,
Then his wife ran off and left him,
so Red went out to look for more.

He figured he could find it on the highway with a rig,
To hear him talk about it, he was going to make it big.

He asked a couple of questions
about how it was 'back when,'
We had all started trucking with iron trucks and men.

I told him about Alaska, the land of the Midnight Sun,
And all the tricks that we had learned
up on that northern run.

We talked about the wrecks we'd seen;
all the drivers we had met,
Some of them were dead and gone,
but some were trucking yet.

We talked about the old rigs: pre-jakes and five by fours;
And how the old suspensions
could shake you out the doors,

...

...

We talked about the Gypsy days
of dodging around the scales,
About the drivers we had known
that spent some time in jail.

We talked about some drivers
who had burnt out on some pills,
About others who had lost the groove
coming down some hills.

Finally we called it quits, for it was time to go;
We knew that we would meet again
somewhere along the road.
The time we had spent together we would do another time,
When fate put us together, further down the line.

I was heading west the other day,
down around San Antone,
I was running hard and feeling bad,
I'd been running on my own;

I pulled into a truck stop for a coffee and something to eat,
I walked up to the counter and took myself a seat.

Just then I thought I heard a voice,
that I thought I recognized,
I turned and saw old Texas Red,
and another bunch of guys.

Old Red, he really looked the part, buckle, boots and hat;
An old coat that said *Auto-car*;
now, where did he find that?   ...

65

...

He told those guys about Alaska
and the roads of ice and snow,
And all the tricks he taught us at fifty-two below.

He told about the wrecks he'd seen
and all the drivers he had trained,
He started giving handles, and even naming names.

He told them of the bad boys,
who had ducked and dodged the scales,
And how the Bears had caught the boys,
and threw them into jail.

He really had them going; they hung on every word,
The waitress even looked at him
 like a cat that had seen a bird.

Then finally he got up and said, "I've got to go."
As he went out through the door,
one kid said, "There goes a pro."

Now, boys, if you'd like some advice
or some help fixing your load,
There are a lot of guys around
who have been out on the road.

But bad advice can kill you; yes, you could wake up dead -
If you listen to the wrong ones like that liar, Texas Red.

We will not volunteer advice, but we'll help you if you ask,
You see, we were once just like you, sometime in the past.

Daddy was a Trucker

Daddy was a trucker; he loved the gypsy life,
Momma was a lady, but she was a trucker's wife.

Daddy, he would phone each night and
      we waited for his call,
Then Momma would tuck us into bed
      and go back up the hall.

No, Momma never cheated, she never even tried.
But I often heard her cuss that truck,
      and many times she cried.

She would sit there in her easy chair,
      and maybe watch a show,
Worried about my Daddy;
      then off to bed she'd go.
She'd sit there on her lonely bed with our old dog and cat,
Then Momma and the good Lord would have a little chat.

She'd tell him about Daddy on the road there, all alone,
Like she was talking to an old friend,
      long distance on the phone.

She'd ask Him to protect him
      out there on the road,
As he went along the highways
      delivering his load

When Daddy would come home,
      at night he'd tell us where he'd been,
All the people he had met
      and the places he had seen,   ...

…

He'd tell about the troubles
      that he'd had out on the road,
He'd swear sometimes that the hand of God
      had helped him with his load.

Momma would just sit and nod,
      but I sometimes saw her smile,

And she knew our Saviour Jesus Christ
      was with him every mile.

Yeah, Daddy was a trucker
      and Momma was a trucker's wife,
And her and Daddy built their life
      around their faith in Jesus Christ.

68

The Trucker and The Bear

A big rig in the darkness, heading east the other night,
Overweight and way behind; his logbook was a sight.

Suddenly, behind him he saw the blue light flash,
The Bear had come to get him and take away his cash.

He pulled up on the shoulder
and climbed down from his rig,
They really had him fair and square;
this fine would be real big.

In the headlight glow he saw her; that little honey Bear,
Her shape divine, her ruby lips, and oh, that golden hair,

She said she had a warrant; was there to take him in,
He just stood there staring, with a big old goofy grin.

She said, "37 women from up and down the line,
Were charging him with broken hearts;
he was going to do some time."

Standing in the courtroom, scared as he could be,
Thirty-seven women; one cop, the judge and he -

The judge said he had been riding high;
wasn't going to set no bail,
The sentence he was handing out
was worse than any jail:

The Judge said, "Look around the room
and prepare to pick your bride.
Your single days are over; in harness you will ride."

...

...

Now he's back out on the highway, taking special care
He has to mind his P's and Q's: he's married to a Bear.

There's those that think an officer would be a lot of fun,
But first you have to realize: she's the one that has the gun.

Advice to a Trucker's Wife

So you're married to a trucker;
      let me give you some advice,
You think this will be easy; well, little girl, think twice.

You will often hear "I love you,"
      and he will tell you this by phone,
Forget about your birthday; you will spend it all alone.

Comes to your anniversary,
      he'll be out there on the road,
He'll spend many holidays delivering his load.

Sure, it has its good points;
      he's never underfoot,
When it comes to supper, there's one less meal to cook.

Learn to like the smell of diesel;
      to him, it is cologne,
It's the first thing that will hit you as he walks into home.

When it comes to children,
      you said you wanted two;
You're the one that will look after them
      when you all get the flu.

The company will lie to him
      and tell him he'll be home,
You'll plan a little party, then spend the night alone.

You will make your little nest;
      get settled in a groove,
He'll find a better company: then he will want to move.

              ...

...

Now I just hit the high points,
        but at least you know the score.
I could go into detail, there are so many more.

I'll just wish you happiness,
        and wish you lots of luck,
By the way, little girl, you're also married to the TRUCK.

Nature's Child

He's a child of the wilderness, a woodsman out of time
Nature is his solace; its stillness fills his mind.

Once he walked with Druid Priests and matched them
        stride for stride,
Once he rode across the plain;
        Cochise was by his side.

He traveled with the Voyagers,
        paddled water deep and cold,
He guided the Forty-Niners
        as they searched for nature's gold.

Even when you're with him,
        it still seems like he is alone.
The wilderness; it calls to him,
        the forest is his home.

Out of step with modern time,
        he does the best he can;
He's out there on the highway,
        a diesel-driving man.

Beneath the jeans and t-shirt, lies the spirit of the wild,
Out of step with modern man, he's Mother Nature's child.

Perception

We struggle from our time of birth, to walk, to talk, to cry;

Always reaching forward, until the day we die.

The wonder in a child's eyes as he perceives a tree,

As he sees an eagle fly, soaring wild and free.

We must take time in our lives, to revisit days of our youth,

Perhaps if we could stand and stare,
                                  we might perceive the truth.

Just Why

I stumble blindly from the truck:
each bone and muscle aches.

Why do I do this to myself?
How much more can I take?

Thirty years of driving;
I've hauled them one and all.

Pulled flats and vans and tanks,
pulled loads both big and small.

I've been on time and I've been late;
been early a few times.

The shippers and receivers
are always messing with my mind.

One thing that I don't understand,
does dispatch have a map?

Or do they pick delivery times
out of a damned old hat?

My Child

Walk with me, reach out and take my hand
Talk with me; I will try to understand.

Cry with me; use my shoulder for your tears
Pray with me; I will help you with your fears.

If ever you should need me, I'll be there until the end
I'm not just a Father; I also am a Friend.

God's Gift

Gently I reach out and touch you
as you lie there fast asleep,

I can't believe my feelings –
how can they run this deep?

I hardly even know you; I just met you yesterday;
What is it about you that makes me feel this way?

Tenderly I hold you, I feel your breath upon my cheek,
Holding you and loving you, I hardly dare to speak.

I know you came from heaven, sent by our God above,
A gift that He has sent me, to prove to me His love.

May you always walk in sunshine,
and not know fear or pain,

I welcome you, my grandson;
life will never be the same.

Take My Hand

Put your hand in mine; walk in the wild with me
Put your hand in mine, we will run wild and free.

Come with me to the mountains,
come with me to the sea.

We can make love in the morning
beneath a tall pine tree.

We can make love in the evening
in the wet and shifting sand.

Walk with me on the wild side,
reach out and take my hand.

You say you led a sheltered life, and I can see that's so,
Come and let me teach you the things you wish to know.

Let me teach you of the pleasure
the act of love can bring,

Just reach out and take my hand; no need to say a thing.

Reach out your hand and touch me,
walk in the wild with me,

> Darling, won't you take my hand;
> we will run wild and free.

Connected

Somewhere in the dark of night, a newborn child cries

Somewhere in a lonely bed, another old man dies,

The child faces forward; the future is his prize;

The old man he looks backward; the past is in his eyes.

Yet they are joined together in the brotherhood of man
Both must work together to be the best they can.

The child must look behind him to learn from our mistakes,

The old man must look forward to teach youth
      what it takes.

One is born and another dies; they will not meet each other,

Yet bonded by the sands of time,
      they will still work together.

Perspective

To him it is another trip, one more load to haul
To her it's several lonely nights, waiting for his call.

To him it is a thing of steel that keeps him safe and warm
To her it is a rival that holds him in her arms.

To him it is a place to work, that keeps his family fed
To her it is a mistress that lures him to her bed.

You look at life so differently because of where you stand,
But the future lies before you, and you must face it
      hand-in-hand.

Both must learn a different look;
      see through each other's eyes,
Communication is the bridge that reaches side to side.

For love, it is a river, that gets stronger as it rides;
But we must have the bridges to get from side to side.

Soft Job

We are working seven days a week
about fifty weeks a year,

They tell us it's a soft job,
all you do is sit and steer.

We deliver all the wood and steel,
the groceries and beer…

Yet still it is a soft job,
all we do is sit and steer.

Ain't been home in six weeks;
ate in ninety different dives,

Yet they tell us it's a soft job,
all we do is sit and drive.

The new truck cost a hundred grand,
and it will last about four years.

Still they say we have a soft job,
all we do is sit and steer.

We are the ones that have to work,
so the economy can thrive.

…

...

Oh, but we have a soft job,
all we do is sit and drive.

Perhaps we should all take a rest;
for four days, maybe five,

Maybe then they would appreciate
all those that sit and drive.

I Cried

I was raised in harder times - men weren't supposed to cry;
We had to face our hopes and fears
                    and never bat an eye.

I went to fight in foreign lands; wounded, then I cried,
The tears were not for me –
                    but for the ones that died.

Years later I shed happy tears:
                    you brought me tears of joy,
You handed me our firstborn; that little, baby boy.

A couple of years later,
                    you did it to me again
You handed me a daughter,
                    while you shed tears of pain.

I cried again as the doctor said, "We almost lost your wife.
She must never have another child."
                    I gladly faced the knife.

We have watched our children grow
                    for all these many years
Many times I held you as my shoulder held your tears

I'm still out here on this highway;
                    God knows how hard I've tried,
I wonder if you realize, how many times I cried.

Grey Wolves

A silent northern forest, the moon begins to rise,

The northern lights are flashing, their beauty
    fills the skies,

In the distance I can hear them; a long and lonely howl

All nature stops to listen, gray wolves are on the prowl.

My heart is beating faster as I listen to the sound,

Now others join the chorus, sound comes
    from all around,

What is it in our memory that gives this sound such fear?

Could it be from long ago, from many bygone years?

My mind takes me back in time;
    we huddle around the flame,

Listen to the howling wolf; death is his other name.

My head turns to the heavens; I join them in their song,

Their voices answer softly, with the Grey Wolf I belong.

North and South

Loaded up in Ontario in all that ice and snow,
Awful hard to tarp a load when it's thirty-five below.
Down across the border, the road is white with snow,
This pavement sure is slippery; but the load just has to go.

South along the interstate, my truck is turning white
The ice and snow begins to thaw,
      as I hammer through the night.

Down across the Georgia line
      where warmer breezes blow,
My toes have finally come to life as further south I go.
Deliver down in Tampa, the sun is shining bright,
Slowly crawl into the bunk; I will sleep warm tonight.

Morning comes; I have to load, another run to make
They say I'm headed north again:
      now where the heck's Slave Lake...

Jill

It was a cold and dirty night, rain was pouring down,

I saw her there beside the road; she was miles
    from any town,

Standing beside the highway, afraid and all alone

Hoping someone would come along
    and help her find her home.

I helped her up into the cab to keep her dry and warm,

She was such a little thing; wouldn't do no harm.

I gave her a couple cookies; it was all I had to eat,

She nibbled them so daintily, there upon the seat.

Later on that very night, she climbed into my bed,

She snuggled in beside me,
    strange thoughts ran through my head.

We never did find her home; yet she is with me still,

She's a pretty little puppy; oh yeah - I call her Jill.

The Gift

Have you ever held a kitten and listened to it purr?

Ever held a puppy, gently stroked its fur?

Ever held a baby and rocked it while it slept?

Ever stopped to help a child, held them while
    they wept?

Ever held your lover as they slept safe in your arms?

Ever helped a stranger and kept them safe from harm?

Ever saved a fledgling that tumbled from the sky?

Ever held a loved one's hand as they prepared to die?

Is there any greater gift than love that we can give?

Perhaps this is the very way that man is meant to live?

Different Breed

What is it in a driver that makes us choose this life,

Could we be a different breed,
       that seems to feed on strife.

We were herders with the Romans when they went
       to foreign lands,

Drovers with Marco Polo as he crossed
       the Gobi's sands.

We were, I know, the daring ones that trekked
       across the plains,

We also were the busy ones that built rails
       for all the trains.

Someday we'll push freighters some place
       among the stars,

Picking up a load somewhere
       and dropping it on Mars.

We have traveled every road and path,
       sailed all the seven seas,

We are the ones that never stop;
       we are a different breed.

Dangerous Dan

Now old Dan was in awful shape, as he ran on
        through the night,
Overweight and way behind, his logbook was a sight.

Now he was turning seventy-plus when he
        hit the Ohio line
He thought the bears were sleeping, that
        everything was fine

Now down the road sat Smoky Joe, that big old
        full-grown bear,
No one had reported him; they hadn't seen him there.

Our Dan was running seventy-two when
        the lights began to flash,
Old Smokey Joe had caught him,
        he was about to lose some cash.

Thirty days thereafter, Dan stood before the Judge,
He claimed that he was innocent,
        on that he would not budge.

"The shippers and the receivers: they are the ones to blame,
They don't allow us any time; they play a little game:
The drivers all throughout the land
        have cheated and have lied,"
Our hero Dan was adamant, "It isn't fair!" he cried.

...

...

The Judge, he sat there quietly,
      and listened to Dan caw;
Finally he raised his head, "I'll tell you about the law -

No one made you cheat or lie; no one made you speed.
The person here that is to blame
      is the man that done the deed.

I'll take away your CDL;
      you're the one that is to blame.
When it comes to law, my friend,
      that's how we play the game."

Later at the truck stop, he tried to clear his name.
Upon the drivers gathered there,
      he tried to lay the blame:
He somehow failed to understand, and never even saw
That no one in the truck stop
      had made him break the law.

The moral of this story about Dan and all his kind:
If you can't afford to pay the price,
      then just don't do the crime.

Wreck

A Texas bumper in the grass, a slowly spinning wheel;
Once a driver's pride and joy is now broken glass,
     and twisted steel.

Smoke is rising from the wreck, the stench of diesel
     is in the air;
Despite the danger to ourselves,
     we get him out of there.

Alas, he died on impact;
     there's nothing we can do.
Cover him with a blanket; shield others from the view.

A family's dream is shattered
     as their lives are torn apart.
One second's inattention
     has stilled a beating heart.

Parents weep for their son; a wife cries for her mate,
A little baby boy and girl think daddy's running late.

And those that tried to help him,
     will go back to the game

But our love for the highway will never be the same.

Wonder

I roam across the nation from sea to shining sea

The highways and the byways are old,
    old friends to me.

Across mountains and across plains, through forest
    and shifting sand,

I never cease to wonder at the glory of this land.

The beauty of a sunset, the power of a storm

The beauty of this nation makes me
    glad that I was born.

The vision through my windshield
    shows the beauty of this land,

A land of peace and plenty,
    touched by God's mighty hand.

Northland

North towards the barrens on a highway
     flanked by pine

The stillness reaches out to me, calls within my mind

I see the mountain vistas, the valleys dark and deep

It somehow reaches out to me, even as I sleep.

North with the forty-niners in their endless
     search for gold,

I seem to know their every trail, their stories yet untold.

They huddled around their campfires in nights
     of bitter cold,

Fought their way ever northward
     in their futile search for gold.

Their bones lie scattered by the trail
     where they died along the way.

When man does search for riches,
     there is a price to pay.

This trail once fraught with danger,
     we cross with ease today,

Yet still within the north woods, there is a price to pay.

...

93

...

This land so harsh and beautiful, where the wolf is
     still the king

Can reach out and touch your soul - and can make
     your spirit sing.

It calls to the lonely, who still feel the urge to roam

The ragged edge of the northland,
     the wolf and I call home.

Scattered

His ashes scattered to the winds but his memory
    still lives,

Though he is dead and gone he still has much to give.

His attitude, his love of life, his sense of right and wrong,

The strength of his convictions helped him
    as he traveled on.

Passed down to all his children,
    this guide still stands strong.

Though he is scattered to the wind,
    his memory lives on.

Montana April

April in Montana, the rain is white and cold

Is spring around the corner; has it been placed on hold?

The highway is turning white;
　　　　my windshield wipers freeze

Mother Nature seems so fickle, why is she such a tease?

Buds are on the willow trees; geese are headed north

Prairie grass is turning green
　　　　new growth is bursting forth.

Spring in all her splendor, struggles to be born;

Farmers waiting patiently, to plant their wheat and corn.

Nature sends a reminder: she is the one in control,

Wind and snow sweep across the land
　　　　and the tumbleweeds roll.

The Mistress

The highway is a mistress that has a heart of steel

She's a part of every driver that ever held a wheel

For some she is a lover, for them she plays a role

For others she's a demon that steals away their soul.

Away from friends and family, drivers have their needs

This temptress of the highway: on their loneliness
    she feeds.

The rig that he is pushing becomes his closest friend,

The wanderlust within him won't let his journey end.

He's coming home so seldom, the family grows apart.

It's hard for those that love him
    to hold him in their heart.

But those that really love him; those that really care,

Will find a place within them and keep him
    sheltered there.

The highway is a mistress, but she can never be a wife.

The love of friends and family is the driver's
hold on life.

Winter

Next year I think I'll hibernate

In the middle of October

Stay in bed till March 15th

When winter should be over.

Or maybe I could just fly south

With all my feathered friends

Not come back till April

When winter is sure to end.

No; I'll just keep on driving

Facing all of winter's woes

I could not appreciate summer

Without facing winter's snows.

Last Kiss

Walk with me in the sunlight and hold hands like
when our love was new

Stroll with me down memory lane together;
me and you.

Sit with me by the water with your shoulder
next to mine,

Let's sit there and remember the passages of time.

Talk to me in the fading light, of all our hopes and fears;

Remember all the things we said over all
these many years.

Hold me in the darkness and promise not to grieve,

Kiss me as I slip away, when it's time for me to leave.

Scatter my ashes on a mountaintop
beneath a tall pine tree,

Let me hear the voice of God as the wind blows
wild and free.

Walk along the beach with me; lovers, hand-in-hand,

Let us leave our footsteps on nature's shifting sands.

King Cat

Through a dark and silent forest a shadow seems to slide
Not a twig is broken, so quiet is his glide.
Sunlight through the branches lights the beauty of his hide
Silent as a thistledown his measured hunting stride.

Nine feet long from nose to tail, and teeth of pearly white
Claws designed to hook and hold
        while he makes his deadly bite.

A quiet majestic beauty and muscles like coiled bands,
Hunter of the high country; how noble he stands.
And then a silent rush, a leap, a strike, a flash of teeth
A deer is downed in seconds - his dinner lies at his feet.

Purring like a house cat, he goes about his feast
A creature made of sudden death, beauty and the beast.

Just Tonight

Come to me in the evening, in the gentle misty light

Let me hold you tenderly at the very edge of night

Kiss me in the moonlight as the moon rides a purple sea

The moon rises with our passion, our souls rise
wild and free

Join with me in the darkness as the moon shyly
hides his face

Our love will know no boundaries, know neither
time nor space

Let me hold you tenderly, see the starlight in your eyes

Let this night last forever, let time just pass us by ...

Kiss me in the morning, in the daylight bright and new

Hold my hand and walk with me in the early morning dew

Darling, spend this night with me
with the moon and stars above

As the entire world sleeps thru the night
we will join in love.

Reflections in a Child's Eyes

Reflected in the bumper, I see a man of steel

A man that spends so many hours behind a steering wheel.

I see the B.C. Mountains and the rocks of Newfoundland,

The swamps of Louisiana and the California sand.

I see the many loads he pulls,
    from clothes to steel and wood

The food and drinks he carries, I'd help him if I could.

I see a man that ties a load with hands as hard as steel,

And yet he can hold me, and know just how I feel.

I see a man who's raising me, to know good from bad,

I see a very special man, that man I call my Dad.

Forever

My darling, won't you come with me

Walk barefoot in the dew

We'll make love in the morning

While the day is fresh and new.

My darling, won't you run with me

Where the wind blows wild and free

We'll make love in the afternoon

In the shade of an old oak tree.

My darling, won't you fly with me

While the moon burns warm and bright

We'll make love so tenderly

In the middle of the night.

Darling, when our time is done

And we must ever part

Know that I will carry you

Forever in my heart.

Notes about the author

Dave Madill is a long-haul trucker who's been on the road for over 25 years. An outdoorsman with a love of nature and former serviceman, most of all he's a father, grandfather and a husband. He says himself he's one of the men who would never be noticed (except when he drives by in his big rig), but he's delivered everything that can fit on a semi-truck and a few things that didn't. If a road goes there, Dave's been there – and he's been many places where there were no roads.

Reflections Thru My Windshield (Part One) is his first collection of poetry which shows the experiences of someone who's seen more places and more miles than most people have ever dreamed about – he's walked the slums of our cities and the tops of mountains and everywhere in between. Dave has held an accident victim in his arms as that person breathed his last, and twice attended the birth of a child on the side of a highway. As such he has a different perspective of the world we live in, and this shows in his writing. Dave is simply a man who writes what he feels and his smiles and tears come through in his writing to give his reader a view of life which most people seldom see. His words have the power of a diesel engine and the touch of an Angel's wing, causing people to stop and take another look at the world we live in and the people around us.

Write Up The Road Publishing has optioned Dave Madill's second and third books of poetry.

Printed in the United States
46026LVS00002B/61-264

9 780976 687214